How To Paint
Fireworks

Laura Jayne Friedlander

To Paul
With gratitude for
inspiration
Best wishes

Laura Friedlander
Dec. '13

Indigo Dreams Publishing

First Edition: How To Paint Fireworks
First published in Great Britain in 2012 by:
Indigo Dreams Publishing
132 Hinckley Road
Stoney Stanton
Leics
LE9 4LN

www.indigodreams.co.uk

Laura Jayne Friedlander has asserted her right under the Copyright, Designs and Patents Act 1988 to be identified as the author of this work.
©2012 Laura Jayne Friedlander

ISBN 978-1-907401-82-4

British Library Cataloguing in Publication Data. A CIP record for this book can be obtained from the British Library.

Designed and typeset in Palatino Linotype by Indigo Dreams.

Cover design by Ronnie Goodyer at Indigo Dreams.

Printed and bound in Great Britain by Imprint Academic, Exeter.

Papers used by Indigo Dreams are recyclable products made from wood grown in sustainable forests following the guidance of the Forest Stewardship Council.

**For my children…
and their children….**

"A poem is intrinsic and natural to the human being ..."

Liz Lochead

There are so many people to say thank you to; my parents, for always believing that this book would come to fruition, my darling children who are a constant source of pride and inspiration, to Ronnie and Dawn for their unending patience!

And to the many poets I have met along life's highway, you all deserve thanks and praise.....

CONTENTS

LAND

LOVE

LIFE

How To Paint Fireworks

LAND

Way of the Storm

Who knows the storm's ways?
Or can tell the waves height
Who sees the sailor's sight
Which sea creature grants him grace?
The heavens give him each day
a journey by stars or candlelight

Who could set the compass right
Or give the ocean praise?
For strength and wit to use
Their steadfast, sturdy faith
Who never thinks to lose
And hauls with every breath
To grasp the life they choose

And meet with victory death.

The Dark Lighthouse Keeper

There is a boat, drowning in the water.
I keep watching, I am the only one who knows, I can see
I am standing on the rocks, nothing can capture me now.

Let the storm come, let the waves crash
Let the foam spew up its waste, then suck it back
To digest all over again.
Let the unnamed creatures of the deep rise to collect you.
They will not take me, for they cannot see that far
I shall always haunt the shore
The flecks of foam that touch my white skin
Like the spittle of ghosts

Let the wind howl louder
Louder than crying my heart out
Let the sky turn black with night
The clouds blacker still, releasing their rain filled fury.

The storm will pass by me, but for you
It is just beginning.
I love and live for the storm.
I am here for the storm
All that temper caught up in the element
It is my expression.

Now, this is your storm.
Like the siren, I lured you to the rocks
I felt the gentle wash of your embrace,
Then felt you beat against me.

The constancy of time may smooth over
All the little cracks
Where you may have split me open.
My light – a blade – as sharp as the salt taste
A flash as stinging as the Poison Fish quill
My brightness may blind you

You shall never speak of the storm
As it drags down my secrets

Rain

Today it has rained like people
Thin and newly alive
Then thick, heavy and old
The water came down like places
A drizzle of beaches
A deluge of mountains
A flash flood of far away
It has been wet like feelings
A thunderstorm of hurt
A cloudburst of ache
Torrential memories.

I Stand Between Weathers

Weather does not arrive in straight lines
the curve of the rainbow is a bent signal
it fades as its colours turn to black
the circle is never complete
I stand between storm and calm
between mist and the lift of clouds
I stand, a backed up wall
against the rain
watching with a slant eye
the run-off down the hill
The fall out later
This peat moor
like the tear stained face
of a worker who has suffered loss
I stand between hurricane force and maritime flag
arguing with the gale
I stand on the shore
wishing I could have the strength of rocks.

Beached

Lying on a rock
A baked stone nest
A sacrificial altar for a mermaid

Sea in the distance
Gulls above, water below
Sunlight, too bright inside my eyes

Skin on Skin
Like two waves lapping
Grains of sand, separate and together

A body as warm and close as the day
A love as long as the waves
That roll in

Now or later
Tide will turn
I will be changed.

Anchored To You

You are like the sea are you not?
I am corkscrewed on these waves
I can only watch as you are fathoms deep
I am hurled against a hull of my life.

You are as fluid as the swell
that reaches then dips
A crest that breaks over my feelings
same in my heart

Pray that my tears will
Never break upon these rocks

You never come in as grey as this
your eyes are the sunlit sea
the seventh wave is your rarity

But...you do keep me safe
When life turns
South'ard
I am anchored to this love
You take me with you
Running ahead of the storm

Your strength, your wisdom
Your arms stretched in a bed
as warm as this is cold
I am lifted up by you,
carried to the shore.

Still It Snows

The snow rolls along the horizon
  dropping onto the sea
  under the curve and curl
  of the clouds.

We find a treacherous spot
where the tide race tells lies
rocks like retracted claws
wait in the cat's snarl of waves

Today we look at life
through a different lens,
extended,
making a monochrome security
weather and paper

Fighting the drowning
clutching at rafts
to make memories

Sky of pearl or pewter

still it snows.

Charcoal and Grey

I will draw a line here
like charcoal
where black sky
meets grey sea
or a reverse
blended with oil sticks
and messy memories
fingers curled into the waves
I see the sea
coming at me
the shore tugging at my feet
And fathoms
that I fight against
never to go under
I am waiting for time
While time waits for me
before I draw the line
to wash the sea across this page

Cliffs are made for Fear

God pulled them up
out of the sea
like dough in his fingers
stretching, kneading
then froze them
to frighten you.
He teased the tops
of the jagged rocks
formed carved heads
of sea monsters
gave them a home
in the waves
that were made
to worry you
to make you think
or let you know
that everything is deeper
than it looks.
We colour our lives
black to make our moods
white waves
waiting for weather lines
like a drawn frown
on printed maps

Friday Night Storm

He rolls in with the storm
I welcome him
the minute he comes along
wild, inspired
Tonight I need his poetry.
His words are whipping round my head
a force ten is lifting the roof of my heart
I am bent double with missing him
walking into the howling
salt spray in the air is throwing
my tears back in my face
If there are going to be icicles
they will be his fingers
stroking my throat
the very rage of these feelings
yet I seek out the storm
for in the eye of it
we lie beside each other
at peace

LOVE

Shiny Fish

The best ones always get away
the ones you fancy
never fancy you.
If you can bait one of these
silver glinting fish
they slip slide
through your fingers
quickly out of your life
back to the fast flowing rivers
they came from.
Or you might be lucky enough
to catch one –
keep this fish in a jar
watch him beating his head
against a glass wall,
watch him sometimes soar
to the surface of your life
more often than not dive
to lie in wait in your deep emotions.
These shiny fish
their eyes are cold
they give nothing away
their mouths are always open
but their mouths don't talk
only their constant swimming tells you.

Roller Coaster

He is my roller coaster love
The waiting
the long climb
leaves me exhausted
Tearful with the fear of fear
Of seeing
what I did not want to see
Over the edge
The drop

He is there
The rush – the suddenness
His breath on my neck
his smile, his being near me,
around me
with me, inside my being

I am scared, I am lonely
I see only the thin framework
wonder what there is
to support the weight of all this
what can hold us up

He is there
He is holding me, kissing me
locking us into this thing
at once so fragile…
so strong, if held the right way

I see him laughing
behind his eyes
he can make this thing sail or fly
He can flip it head over heels
make it spin

His eyes are as blue as the sky above
There is no getting off the roller coaster
We are staying for the whole ride

When it slows we are comfy

We got carried away
so happy
He looks at me
Says 'Trust me – you are safe"
Back on the ground
Look at this thing
that loops the loop
I will always bring you back
The roller coaster
does not go anywhere
Look at me
Listen to me!

I am not going anywhere
Not leaving you

Winter Barley

Now your thoughts look forward
to the coming of winter barley
the stem that has ripened
In the once bare field.
I look back to the early spring days
when seeds were first planted
growing warm in the earth.
In my head a hope
you forming me in your hands.
The line that your finger drew
around the curve of my face
the way the lines of barley grew
in the big field
your rough hands tender on a soft mound
of earth
or flesh.
The birds who dipped to look
then knew to leave well alone
the stalks of barley, Ah,
everything parting
to let us through.

Where Shall I Sleep?

Even though we share the same bed
I sleep alone
I think that the cornflower blue
Of cotton sheets
Should remind me
Of the lazy haze of Summer.

Now I can only feel
The crumpled, quilted landscape,
The torrential heat of feelings
A land slide of emotions;
The subsidence of dreams.

When Words Fall

When words fall from you
they are pieces of the rock that you are made of
breaking off and hitting
     my head and my heart
They hurt
They graze and cut
Words that roll me
back and forth
along the rocky shore of feelings and thoughts.

On warm days I press my spine
against the crumbling sandstone of you
I stand in front of you
when the storm comes
while the rain pelts the broad granite of you.

We are the Poets

We are the poets, you and I
    We are ugly and evil
In the early morning we go out
from high places to land on ragged rocks
like crooked cormorants or shags, indistinguishable,
scanning the surface to discover what lies beneath

In the afternoon we stretch our wings on the sand
rolling new words along,
like stones beneath our feet,
uncovered as the tide pulls back
from a sudden found shore

In the dark we crawl back to our lairs
a tear in the cliff face
we do not sleep
we lie in wait…

Hiding From Myself

Today I am hiding from myself
I go among crowds
When they smile their widest
then I hide in back alleys
I talk too loudly
laugh too much
on the way home
I walk to the water's edge
almost into the sea
but not quite
I lick my lips
Cannot tell
salt spray or tears
is this vision
A blurred horizon
the future

Thorns

You were going to come to me
With the expectation of spring
A pregnancy of excitement and boisterous joy.

Leaves unfolding, the curl of new growth
The blossoming fullness of hope.
I was waiting......waiting.....

On the way home
My thoughts rose over the tops of trees
Corn fires, a blazing harvest
Black stubble fields
Now as bare as my eyes

You were shining bright
As the liver red of berries
Then plucked away to feed memories

I left, feeling the thorns of autumn.

There in Black and White

Now I am a modern girl
watching the black pen of time
race across the white page
No two moments are the same,
yet nothing has changed
Slaves to work
Slaves to the nation
and you are always
my master.
My mind may be far away all day
but in those frightening nights
it returns to you forever
My history has clung to shades of grey
between black and white wars

Red Walls

The Red walls
Run down on us
Trickle on to the thin bed

We, drinking a devil's brew
Seal our lips
No word to anyone
Baring Souls

The red room
Where our ghosts cannot enter
Out of sight
Out of mind
A stolen, lying night

Windows turning black
Traffic passing the door
On the narrow streets below
At the back of my mind.

Nightshift

I worry about you
working nights in a cold shed
where the bare bulbs
cast a ghostly light
that blues the skin,
where the white walls
suck at your soul
and the stone floors
absorb your memories
so that they never more
issue from your mouth.

I worry that outside the walls,
the small hours
are too dark for you
that the journey is too long,
the path back home is too narrow.

I wonder if the sea
is too grey for you,
your thoughts too deep,
the wind too harsh,
the cold too stinging.

I care, that you need to see summer
to be lifted up, heavenward.
I care, that time is short
so I shall wait at the factory gates for you.

Remember Me
(For Melvyn Bragg)

Last night I threw *Remember Me* into the sea
Apologies to Melvyn Bragg
but he has a lot to answer for
There are some days
when you just have to
throw some words away
memories too
carried off in the tide race
swirled in the firth
Praying I was,
that the tide was going out
way out
like that love
A storm whipped up
squalled
then shushed away
not long ago
nor lasted long
now grazed on shingle
tears washed out to sea.
"The novel tells the story
of the entire affair," he said
How right he was
I knew from the first page
sorry,
it could never be more than fiction.

Breath of Ghosts

Does the breath of ghosts
Rustle the leaves already?
So early in the day,
So early in the year?

Spirits petrified in wood
White in places
And yet may turn to coal.

The stones lined up
To read out
The names of souls

Who once fed their families
The children who grew so fast
Like weeds
Around their feet

In between the smooth grass
The rough grass
The lines that separate
And rest for tiny birds
That cross such great divides

The robin at your head
Seems misplaced
Because we all assume
He must come at a cold grey time
Today is too bright we say.

We can laugh in the sun
And while you may sing
Don't remind us now of winter.

The hot spot burned on your breast
Baked blood
Sitting on the veins of trees
Branches, bleeding shoots from their tips.
We all start to grow again.

Table of the Elements

This table of the elements
carved glass in the grey of the sea
is the wind and rain
snow and ice
of an old life made new

formed from ancient things
a surface reflection
a water droplet
sand and stone back and forth
stone, sand.

Stones Words Sand

What of the mighty cliff face
that rose above us,
that became a rock?
Do the sea gulls eat stones?
Do they stick in their gullet?
Would the stones come from a deserted shore?
Every word I want to say to you
           may be like those stones –
carefully chosen, picked over and sifted,
sorted for size, shape and feel
then judged
           to see which ones will be dull
           and which may shine.
I am thinking of you
           never let the words be ground down
to grains of sand
           slipping through our teeth
dried on our lips
blown away by a breath
of sea breeze cast to the ocean.

Soul Mates by the Shore

Sitting on a rock
at the narrow harbour entrance
sheltered from the wind
rolling in from the Atlantic
the terns in unison
their dipping flight
their partnership for life
I am thinking of you
I look out to sea
You are with me
a message that I could send
across the water
or sing into the wind
I know it will find you
for this is love poetry
The white wave crests
will paint out all the wrong words
and leave just what you need
to hear
tears gone away
blended into a salt spray
I can almost feel your hand
on my shoulder
as I stand at the edge
you are the lookout
my heart swells
I am full of you
Our song is endless
as this sea.
How can I explain
as the tide rolls on
that this nature is within us
Soul mates

At the End of August

Last night I could
have shown you Mars
made a thousand wishes
on a thousand stars
I could have kissed you then
in the dark of night
and hoped and prayed of when
I might just might
have told you
how I really feel
this passion, it's true
yet somehow surreal
I could have talked
to you
whilst this park
waved as it knew
where we walked
while the leaves in the dark
still gripped my flimsy dreams
or the secrets they had seen
all hopes bursting at the seams
I could have held you on and on
under a lonely tree
forgetting guilt or doing wrong
separate or together
perhaps a thought
of you and me

Six Feet Six

Clutching, clawing
Behind Bars
Tangled in your clothes

You cannot even stretch
Taught against the walls

Mind screams against it all
The belt lashings
That bring sun and sea
Wind and rain

Distant memories across your brain
Now you know you can never escape
The pain of confinement

A bird
Blown across your window
May be a scrap, waste paper
You can no longer imagine freedom

Six foot six, in a six foot cage.

River Afternoon

We walked down to the river
where swans slowly drifted
on a lazy afternoon

We watched, we waited
while the sky marked the hours
the hill, the meadow
became our house, our bedroom

We crossed each other's bodies
like the winds from some far horizon
from a land that brought
only mystery and sand

We said we would love forever
we both knew we had lied
The swans bowed their heads
dipped their necks into the water

They wept into the river
the trees waved their branches
in sad surrender or farewell
the breeze whispered –

'Dreams are just for dreamers
Plans are just for schemers; can't you tell?'

Remind Me

Remind me of all
I was going to say to you
in the morning
All the thoughts I had
laid out for you
when I was watching the sea
from a snow framed window
tracing a line on the glass
like a tear on a face
Remind me to wait
not to give in to the rip
but cling tight to the lines.
Remind me as
the grey painted night
falls onto the sea
I shall wait
for a winter sun
to tint the clouds
the colour of honey
To warm my day
For you to
remind me again…

Manning the Barricades

I would man the barricades for you
I would be a human shield
I would stand before you
my heart armoured by sinews
that are ropes that tie us together
in thoughts and dreams
our visions of justice of right
our hopeful future

I would protect you
I would be your first line of defence
that Arnhem, that scarred land
that stands a test of time
blood red with memories
years and years of strengthening
like the silt or salt of crystal
that holds a light locked in a prism
within the fortress
behind the barricades

I will be there for you

How to Paint Fireworks

You and I separated
By straits of water or time
Brought back to life an ancient chemistry
Drawn across a black canvas of sky
I saw the sparks fly
Caught in your eyes
I remember you had told me
About mirrors of the soul
In a crowd, as lonely as the hermit
I sought you out
My heart as high as the rocket's soar
A splash of hope against the stars
The shower of colours
Washing the hills clean
I knew an angel was out there
Your golden wings above me
I watched the fireworks
Painting my dreams across the night
I prayed they would stay aloft

Arctic

His hand reaches
to stroke a curl of black hair
from her white face.
Her stare is as cold as the landscape.
He has gathered her in
no capture, sheltered her,
her lips are tinged blue
as the filtered light.
He longs to bathe her
in furs and skins.
He is glad the men have left
for the season
now just two
match sea and sky,
her eyes as deep as the seal pool.
Her mouth does not speak
or tell tales of her abandonment
left to fend for herself
given the name of a dog*.
Seasons change
from constant night to single day;
she stands arms folded
a proud statue
looking from the square panes
of the wooden hut
sees the green valley,
watches him hike away
for just a day
safety.

* In ancient Inuit folklore anyone who had disgraced the tribe was given
the name of a dog then cast out and abandoned to fend for themselves
in the cold.

Dangerous Dance

Sometimes
Your eyes
Still dance a sad dance
The dying swan
When I am at the water's edge

No! A crazy tango
Across the ice

This is not contrived
Nor some pretend paradox
I want to dance

But now
Standing on the bridge
On points
I must tread warily.

Cook's in the Kitchen

She stares at white walls,
knows it is raining outside,
smears that cooled steam
from the glass panes.
When she is angry
she tears flesh
from boiled bones.
When she is missing him
she peels onions,
tears mixed with
salt and longing.
Waiting for him
she bakes bread;
her heart rises and swells.

Eve's Apple

I have come from a garden
that has grown for years long
it comes around
beaten and fallen to the ground
        bruised
a whip lash on your skin
white teeth on white flesh
I do not want this sharp taste
        let it be sweet
The seed is the very core of me
what I bring
will be pruned back
The green of youth
        a blush
The coming of age
        a tart
Hidden in the green leaves
past the purity of blossom
the temptation of
Eve
        becomes
bird pecked
maggot chewed
pig mashed to pulp.

Leaving His Bed

Pulling myself up from the warm sheets
Away from his smooth skin
Drawing back from his breath on my neck
I go out
As the cats are coming home
Silent on the pavement
As the dawn tears strips off the night
As the street lights flicker and give up.
The cold air of Sunday morning
Hits my face like a slap after his gentle kiss.
I head back to another place
The space I have created for us
But without him I wander through rooms
Wrapping my arms around myself
Wishing for him.
He has a bed here too, our bed, not shared enough
There are things to be done
Not now – later
For now I need this solitude
I do not want anything else to intrude
on my thinking of him.
I need to remember the way we were last night
Talking, laughing
Holding him
I stroke my skin
Where the remains
Of the very essence of him
Are still stuck to my flesh
I know in this early morning
He is right beside me.

Cloth

At the quiet time of waking, the day
fell about me like cloth,
wet wool in the morning
fantasy moths
in my dreams had already begun to
chew little holes around the edges.

The new day hung heavy and damp,
the early hours draped their heavy
blankets over hedges and fields
reluctant to give up shape and
shadow to the coming light.

Later, bells rang and tore a hole in the
shroud before lunch,
a tear too ragged to be patched
no seamstress, no healer could be
found to do the work.

Every little hour I was sucked back
to the edge of the tear
the tear in my day – how dare you?

But slowly – after noon
the day became silken and though I
walked behind a veil of hidden
feelings, friendship let me peer
through the mesh.

Evening was lit by flames that sent a
shower of bright sequin sparks
across the black cotton cloth of the sky.

Late at night I settle in to the soft
down of sleep;
a voice comes to me like an old
comforter.

Driving South

He is driving.
We are tied to this black road,
my hand is tight on his thigh
his hand moves too,
slipping through gears,
over riding my thoughts.
He is looking straight ahead.
I dare not turn my head
to look at him
for fear
the tears
lying in wait
will no longer stay
hidden in the past,
but pour out my secrets;
we will both lose our way.

Leaving in November

Dawn
grey of course
comes creaking over the hill.
The trees are bare headed now
their branches like hair and veins.
      A lone crow,
his wings with dirty fingertips
swoops before the headlight beam.
      Cumulous clouds
are seeking out my aching bones.
On the road behind me
there is the house.
A trail of white tissues
tears now dried in,
leads from your room to mine.

Truth is Another Country

Truth is another country
time is the simple sword of honesty
yet we select, we imagine
in theatres of blood
we try to wash our hands
of that which we have spilled.

We create our archives:
the man, the terrible misdemeanour,
the great race,
before we all become drab in the dust
fearful of becoming nothing.

Soldiers say
we must fight the prophets of darkness,
forget the way we are meant to be
or the way we were or could foresee,
grow into Emperors, Conquistadors.

We are sons of the road
casting aside negative images
we cannot shout
we let you think
we wage a war of soft words.

A Little Bit Northern

When I was driving home
heading out the old North Road
in the darkness going back to him
those headlights stinging bright were like tears
that took up such a tiny space on my face
yet he filled my whole world.

He was only three weeks in the north
when the northern lights stole him away one night
a wonderment, he turned his head to the skies,
his heart turned to me.
He had made a northern start
becoming a northern man.
One day no doubt he would be hardened by the hill
or the chill of winter across the firth.
He was bound to make a salt stain on my heart.

Many nights he was in my tattered scraps of dreams
like a ragged crow beating against the wind.
I loved him for all the good of the summer croft,
the harsh weeks of winter.
I knew that through the shriek of a south westerly
I need do far less than shout
like waves we crashed upon the shore
but, when the water was calm, we were together
as myriad as sun spots on a summer sea.

LIFE

Tug Master

Out from the bay
then around the head
the wind whistles him home.
On a bridge above the hull
he is like a painted doll
with Russian red cheeks
hair curled tight to his head
like the Buddha's knot.
The boat crosses the sound,
his life is wrapped in a poem
rolled up in the sea
grey wash against the hulk of his back.

She is waiting for him;
salt fish for tea.

Trawlermen

We wear our work wrapped around
our souls
like wet clothes
coats once warm wool, sodden
while women wait on a bleak shore
with drenched shawls about their faces
strands of hair
like the wrack we dredge up
plastered to their cheeks
greying like the sky.
Here on the deck the colours run
red blue white
blood sea ice
we watch gulls run across the water
leaving their footprints in a white wake.
Around our cuffs
blackened scales that have fallen
from a slick green blue skin
dyed the same colour as the sea
our collars unstitched
ragged from the life,
the way we were hooked.
The fish, their empty eyes
as glass
as the floats
that for many years
have ensnared us all.

The Prisoner's Wife

When they took you away
I saw a ship being cast off
my arms as heavy as wet rope
flung down
my skin like a soaked fleece
weighted.

Blown about as random
as snow in the wind
a pattern melting
tears too wet to settle.

When they took you away
I felt like the scared passenger
in a car parked in the hurricane's path;

I felt like an empty can
rolling down the deserted street
rattling the silence of the night.

I do not know when my joy will return.
These people who separate us
divide our lives
and rule over us.

And this will make me write to you.

The Plait in her Hair

Hair in a plait
Messy
The artist in her head
Whispers around her ears
The pattern of weave.
The wind whips
A strand of thought
Across her brow
Blonde
With grey wisps
Of wisdom
At her temples
The plait in her hair
A thick rope
Of sixties romance.

The Clip

Come May or June
The warmer days
Wind or breeze
Lighter nights
Greater ease
The clip is cast
Off the sheep
The wool thrown down
Over the ground
Inspected and likely as not
Passed unfit
I've seen bales of wool
Thrown over the cliff face

If this fleece had its own mouth
It would tell of the winter
If it had eyes it would see
The storm coming in
Despite the hours of darkness
It would sense
Huddled in the peat bank lea
The snow sweeping over its back
The wind deafening a lambing cry

If this dead fleece clipped off
Could ever feel again
The warmth of the old ewe
The ignorant passion of the ram
The strength and weakening of lambing
Under the fleece
The softest, the finest
The purest, the best yet
New growth.

Small Boats, Big Sea

After the summer
God chooses the time
when the boats are lifted
out of the green brown harbour
before it turns black grey
three months of tin on water
six months of winter
waiting for the winch.
A small boat arrives
cutting across the sound
as fierce as a small dog.
Boats are lined up
their hulls painted
to match the weather to come
storm grey.
Men stand on the jetty
their hard shoulders now soft
sagging with resignation
hands in pockets
the rustle of beer money
softens their sighs.
They give a wave to the crane man
who watches the bow rise
into the air
then back down to rest
a boat out of water
On dry land
the men make a wake
to the boat house

cans of lager
tales of the summer past
and passed around
plans for next season.
Bigger fish
bigger boats.

Leap of Faith

When her man died
she washed his clothes,
hung them, empty now,
to dance on the line.

His windblown boiler suits
hollow breeks for his body
once young and sleek
as she rosaried the prayer bead pegs
and wrestled the twisted lines
of ancient hymns
on a windy day.

She felt the salty needles of tears
stabbing the backs of her eyes
as she watched the shore
sea foam like soap.

When he was cold in his grave
she laid out his clothes.
She thought she saw Jesus
walking on water across Yell Sound*
but it was just the ghost of 'him' –
another trick of the light.

She wore his shirt through the night
though she had ironed out the smell of him
he was still wrapped around her.

She dreamed of Jesus
that he was lost on the hill
but it was just another crofter
who had counted every sheep he had.

His dinner was set out on the table.
She thought she heard Jesus
drive past in a van
but it was just the blue bus travelling north.

* Yell Sound –a treacherous strait of water known for its seven knot tidal race, in the north of the Shetland Isles.

Breeks – old Scots word for trousers

Knitting Socks

I knit with four needles
casting on like starting
a new life
even stitches on three points
a trinity.

Round and round,
making a rib,
turning a heel
from the fleece to the wheel
counting.

I mark time
with four needles
four weeks of the month
four seasons of the year

infant child woman crone
lives knitted together
the rich veins
like skeins
in varied colours.

Knitting a pattern
grafting a toe

all measured.

Young and Old

I move in the world of old men
Old Fathers marking time
Confusing history
And changing it, so they can be always right.
I move quickly, lightly
They only notice a flash of light in the corner
An unimportance in their day.

I can sing of wonder and of things
That old men will never see.
Old men will grow irritable
And pick at strange scabs
Families who can do no right
Finding fault with bones and skin.

I come from the place of young people
Old men cannot understand
I dance in a small space of air
I breathe in the sunshine
I can reappear from other dimensions
A sudden form
A hologram of another life
Liver spotted hands are scared of me.

I can emerge
A new life form
For old men I am like
A cinema-scope special effect
I cannot sink into the grey soup of age.
I am so good
Old men are afraid.

Zion

He climbs the metal stairs
to the loft
complains that these are the wrong steps
everything is wrong these days.
What happened to the unusual ladder
that was one long pole
that went on up
to where he had stored all of Zion?
Wrapped in cases
trunks boxes marked important
shelves that bent with the weight
of responsibility
and ticking minutes,
books never to be read
but words to be saved and dried out.
He starts to search
for the memories of Zion

Righteous in his belief
a sermon on how it is
how it should be
good to store up treasures
at his time of life,
heaven or earth it does not matter.
He's holding on though
keeping the faith,
never disregarding the dogma
that brought him through it all,
two wars and all the rest.
He likes to remember

and remind.
In the dark nothing matches
the silence of the loft
becomes strange
noises no sense.
He fumbles for the light switch
that will change everything
in this place
for the brightness to shed
illumination on it all –
make sense of Zion.

Zealous pictures
photographs haphazard in crates
he claws for the past –
an Aunt all real again
family dust is wiped away
by a dirty sleeve –
he will not fade like these,
grime seeps into his fingers.
He rejoices in Zion.

The Way that I Write

You think that I cannot write
on the dark winter days.

I am sitting on a beach
while the wind blows
words across the page.

Where graphite and sky
are a perfect colour match.

I am climbing the banks
to finish a verse
my fingers turning to a shade of sleet.

I am seeking out
a hollow in the hill
to sit; marking the time
between think and ink.

Indigo Dreams Publishing
132, Hinckley Road
Stoney Stanton
Leicestershire
LE9 4LN
www.indigodreams.co.uk